THERE ARE DADS WAY WORSE THAN YOU

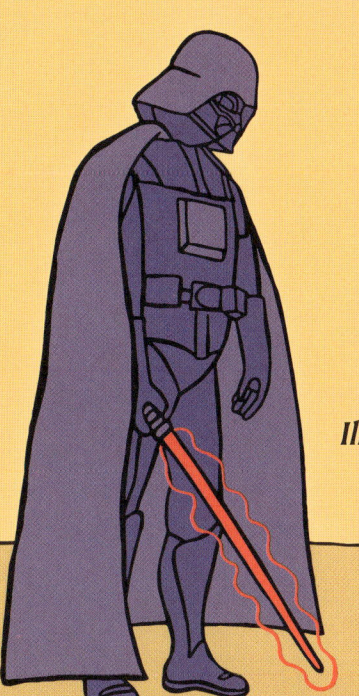

Unimpeachable
Evidence of
Your Excellence
as a Father

GLENN BOOZAN
Illustrated by Priscilla Witte

WORKMAN PUBLISHING • NEW YORK

Copyright © 2024 by Glenn Boozan

Hachette Book Group supports the right to free expression and the value of copyright.
The purpose of copyright is to encourage writers and artists to produce the creative works
that enrich our culture.

The scanning, uploading, and distribution of this book without permission is a theft
of the author's intellectual property. If you would like permission to use material from
the book (other than for review purposes), please contact permissions@hbgusa.com.
Thank you for your support of the author's rights.

Workman
Workman Publishing
Hachette Book Group, Inc.
1290 Avenue of the Americas
New York, NY 10104
workman.com

Workman is an imprint of Workman Publishing, a division of Hachette Book Group, Inc.
The Workman name and logo are registered trademarks of Hachette Book Group, Inc.

Design by Galen Smith
Illustrations by Priscilla Witte

The third-party trademarks used in this book are the property of their respective owners.
The owners of these trademarks have not endorsed, authorized, or sponsored this book.

The publisher is not responsible for websites (or their content) that are not owned by the publisher.

Workman books may be purchased in bulk for business, educational, or promotional use.
For information, please contact your local bookseller or the Hachette Book Group Special Markets
Department at special.markets@hbgusa.com.

First Edition April 2024

Printed in China on responsibly sourced paper.

10 9 8 7 6 5 4 3 2 1

*To my dad,
Tom Boozan,
who let me
climb trees,
watch* The Simpsons,
*and play with matches.
I love you!*

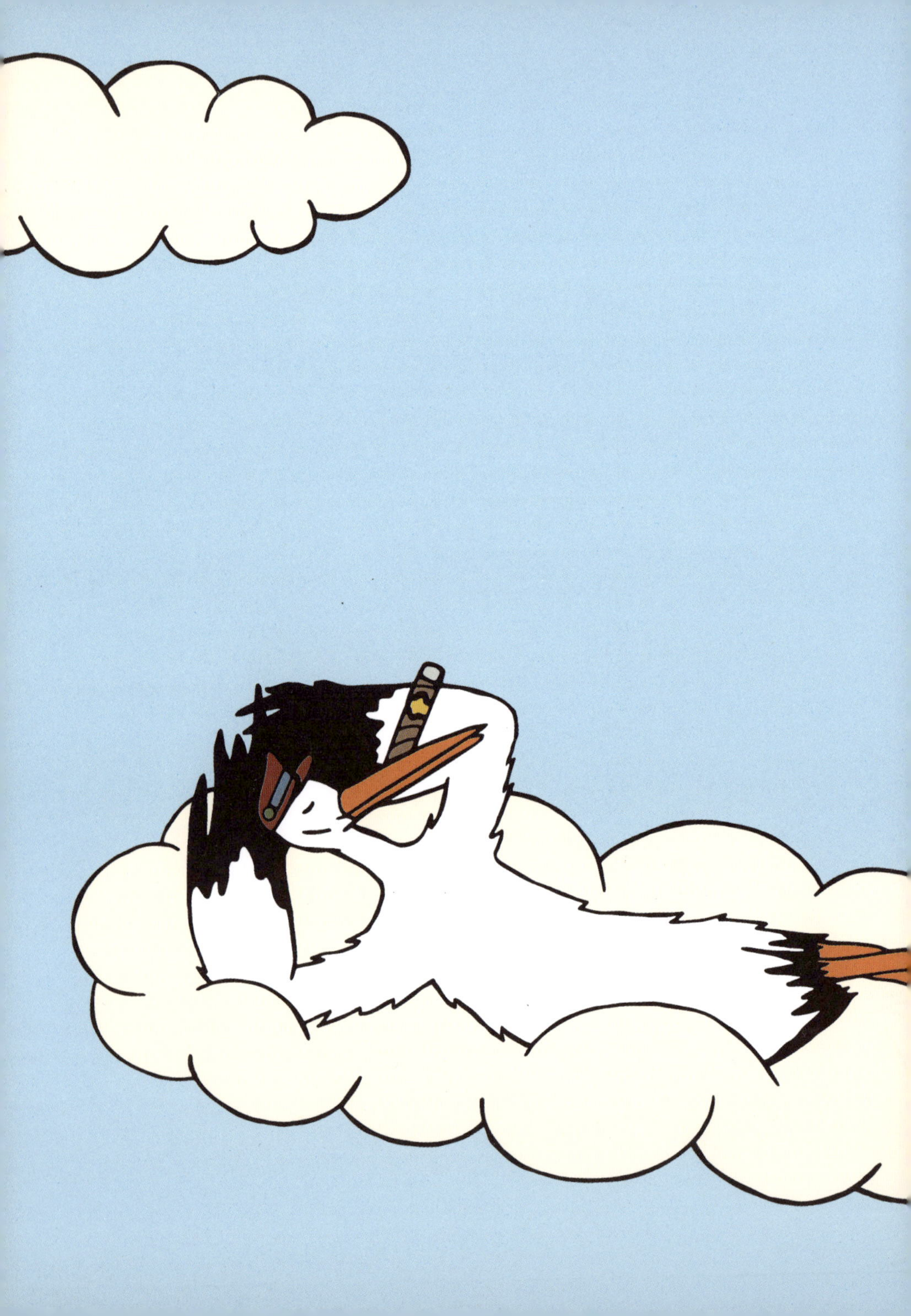

Congratulations, **Daddy-O!**
Welcome to the club.
Who knew that it was possible
to feel **this kind of love?**

As days go by, with pride and awe,
you watch your child grow.
"Fatherhood, **it's so damn good!"**
you'll shout for all to know.

Then, as if by magic,
 comes a **whisper**
 in your ear.

It creeps up slow
 then **grips you tight**—
 that specter we call...

...fear.

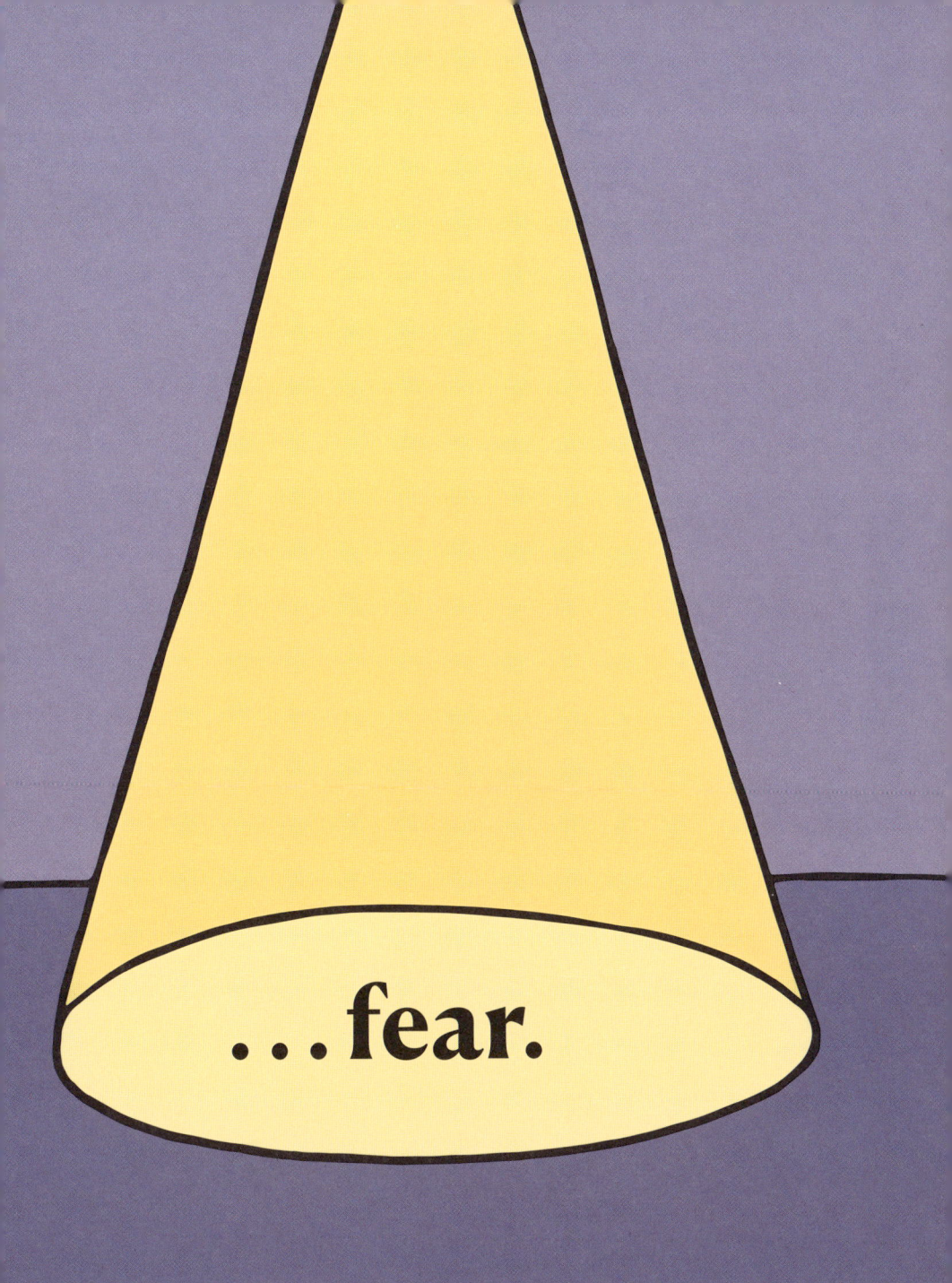

"**What if** I'm not meant for this?"
You might begin to think.

"What if I try this 'Dad stuff...'
and I completely **stink?**"

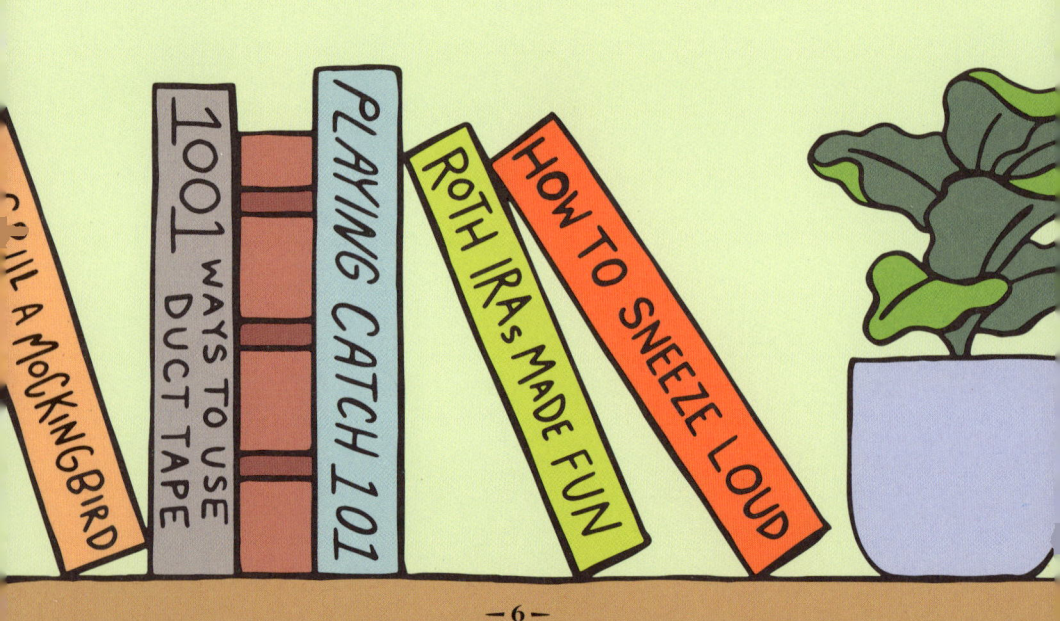

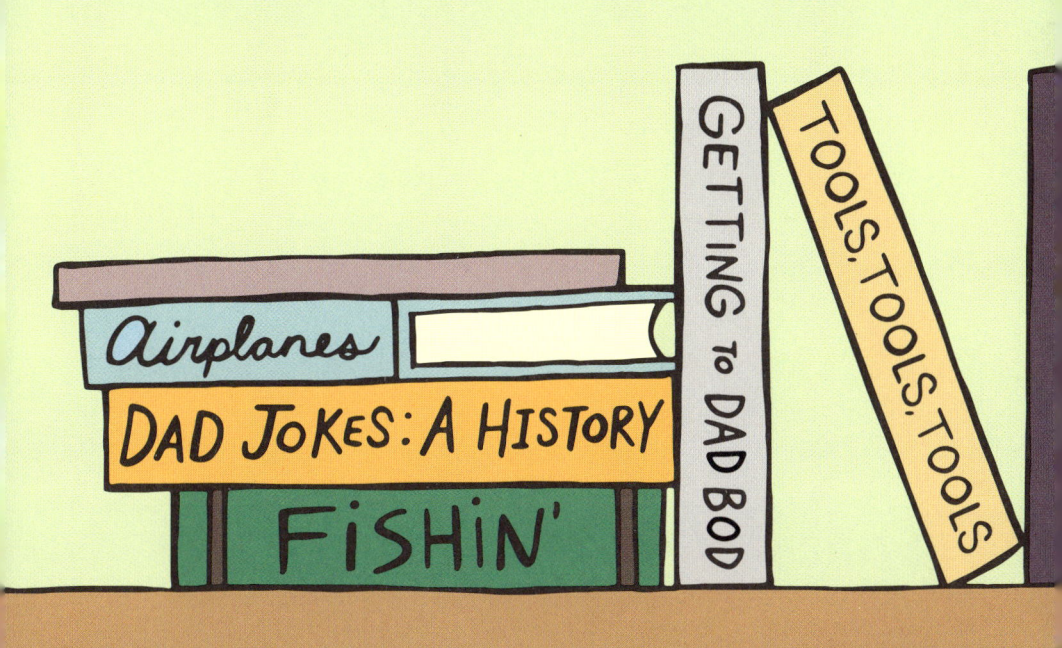

"I can't explain **how taxes work,**
or how to cook a steak.

I don't know facts from
World War II, or when
to check your brakes."

"I've never built **a treehouse**— I haven't even tried."

"What if my kids need something... I simply **can't provide?**"

TREEHAÜS
ASSEMBLY INSTRUCTIONS

And though of course, you **will** mess up, remember this is true:

When put into perspective, there are dads **WAY** worse than you.

You can't be worse than **Thanos.** You know, the purple guy?

He pushed his daughter off a cliff. **So yeah,** you're doing fine.

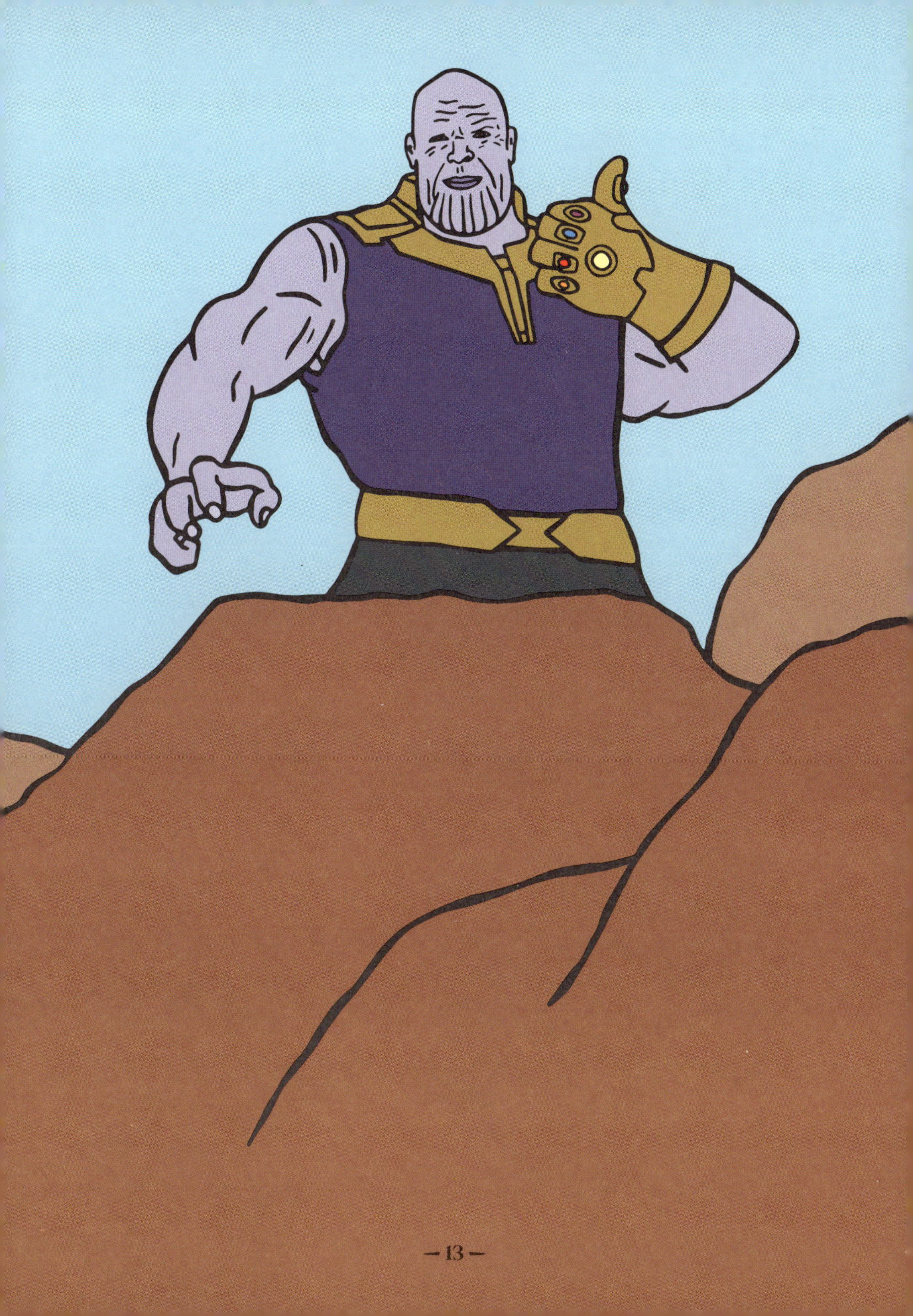

What if, at a barbecue, your **"Grill Dad"** skills are green?

As long as what you're cooking isn't **methamphetamine.**

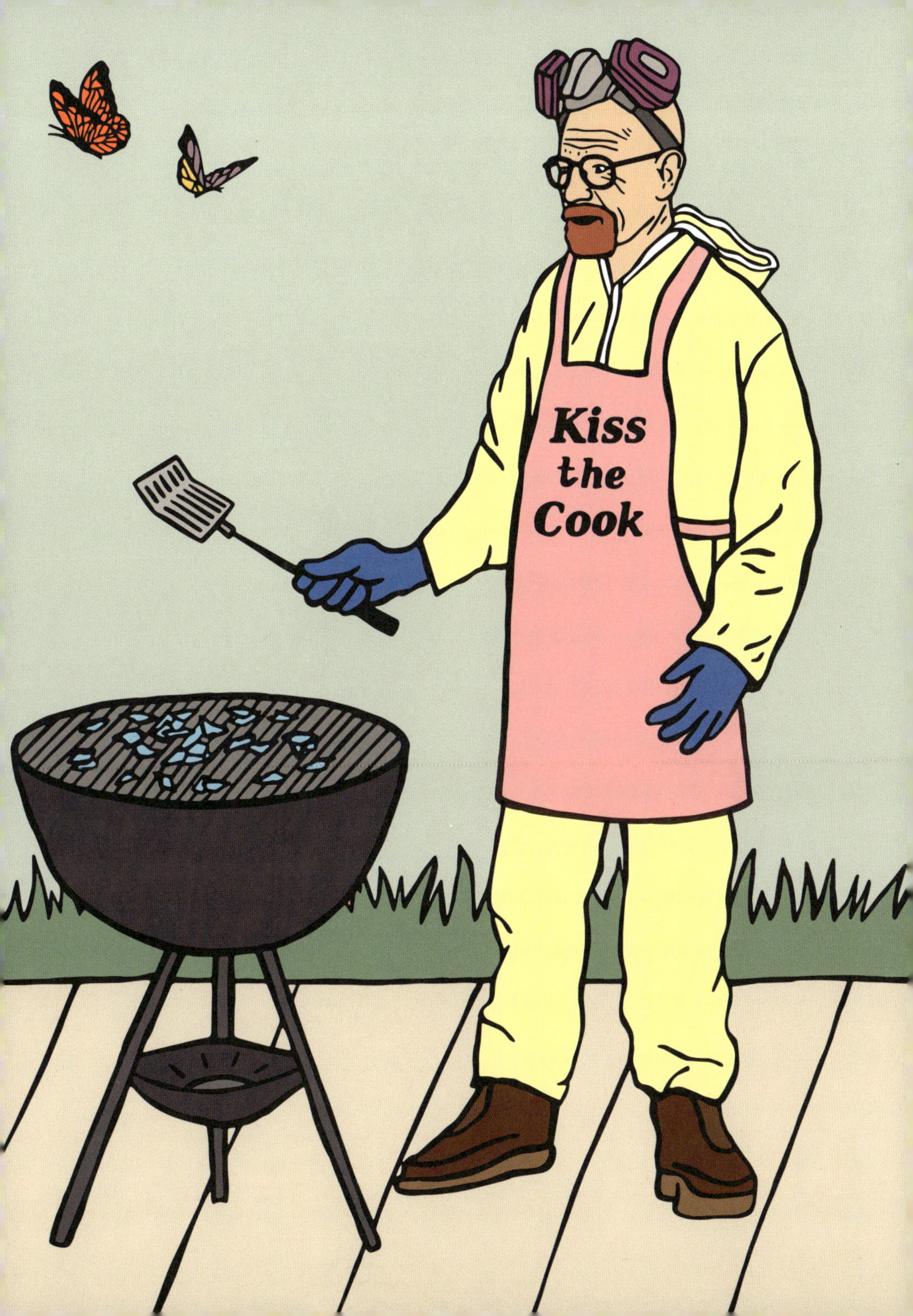
Kiss
the
Cook

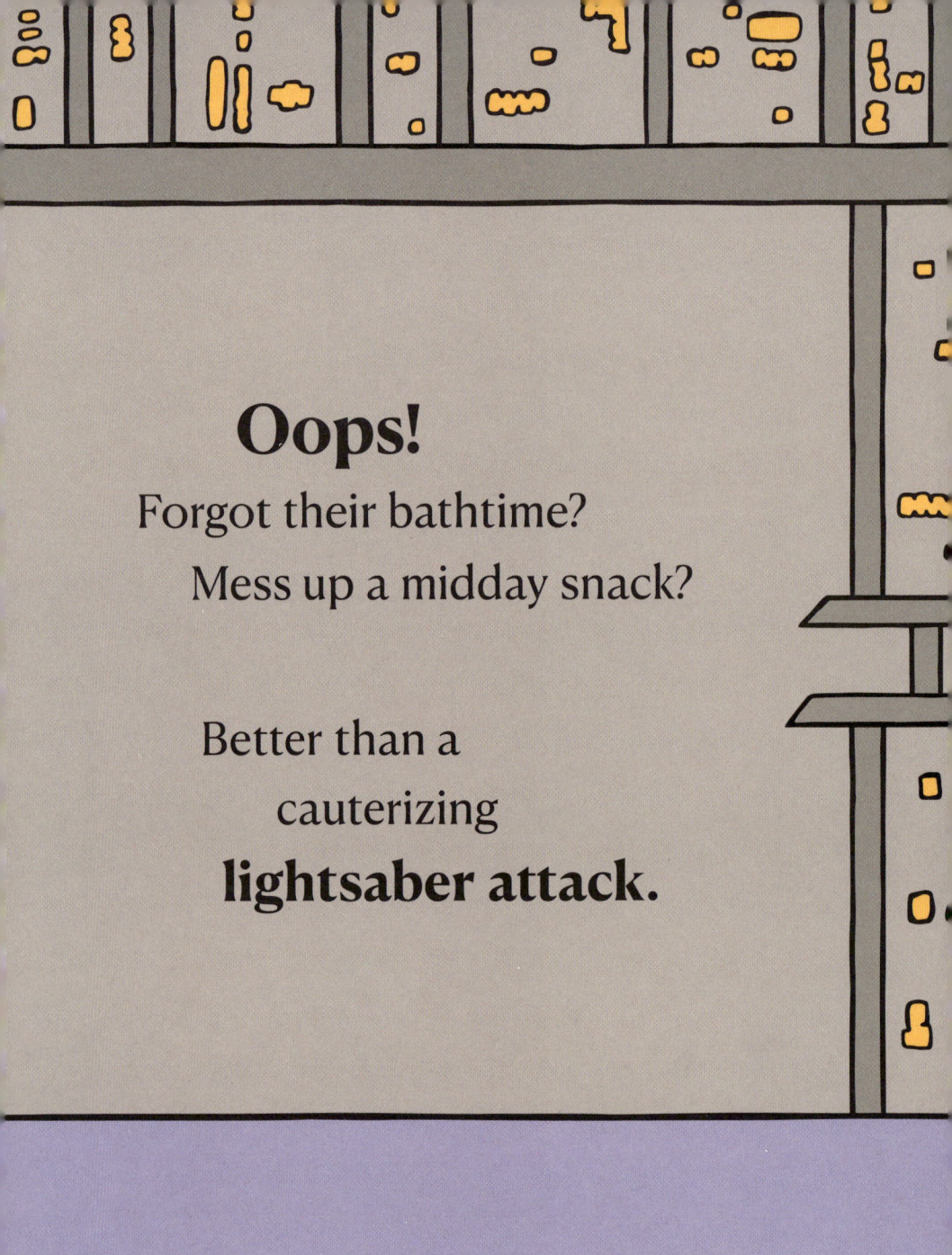

Oops!
Forgot their bathtime?
Mess up a midday snack?

Better than a
cauterizing
lightsaber attack.

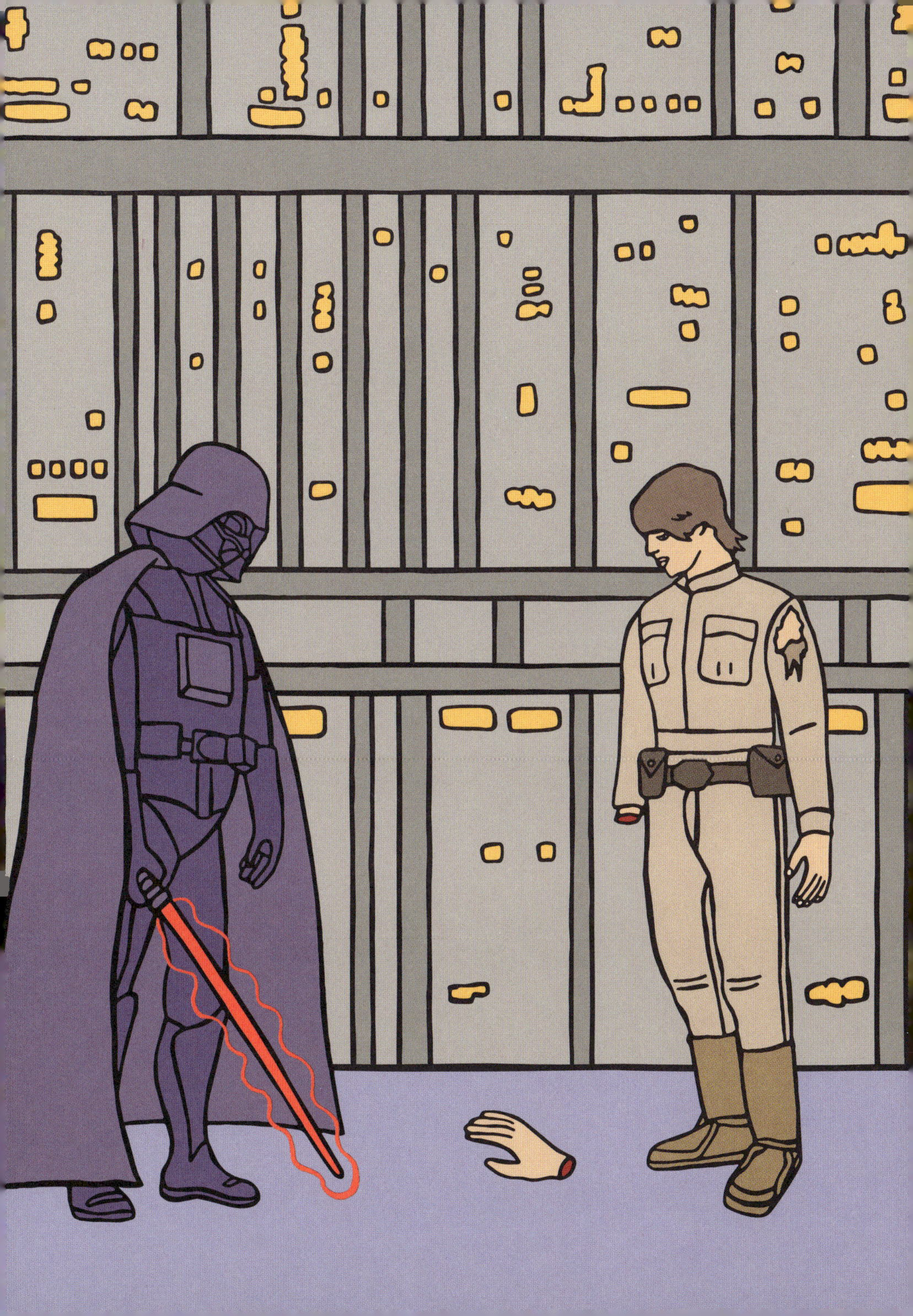

Clever **Doctor Frankenstein** created his own son ...

...who then went on to **murder** everything and everyone.

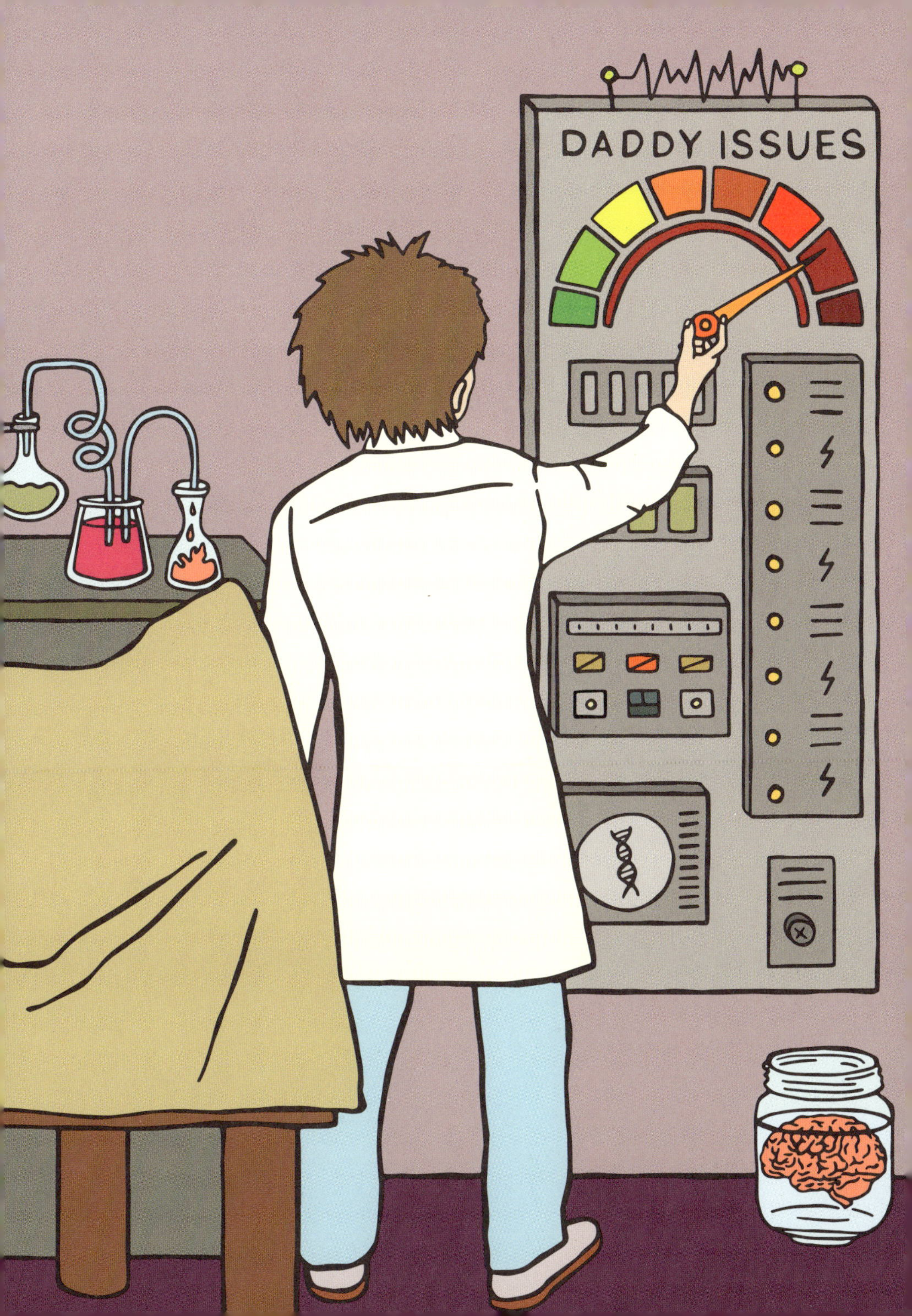
DADDY ISSUES

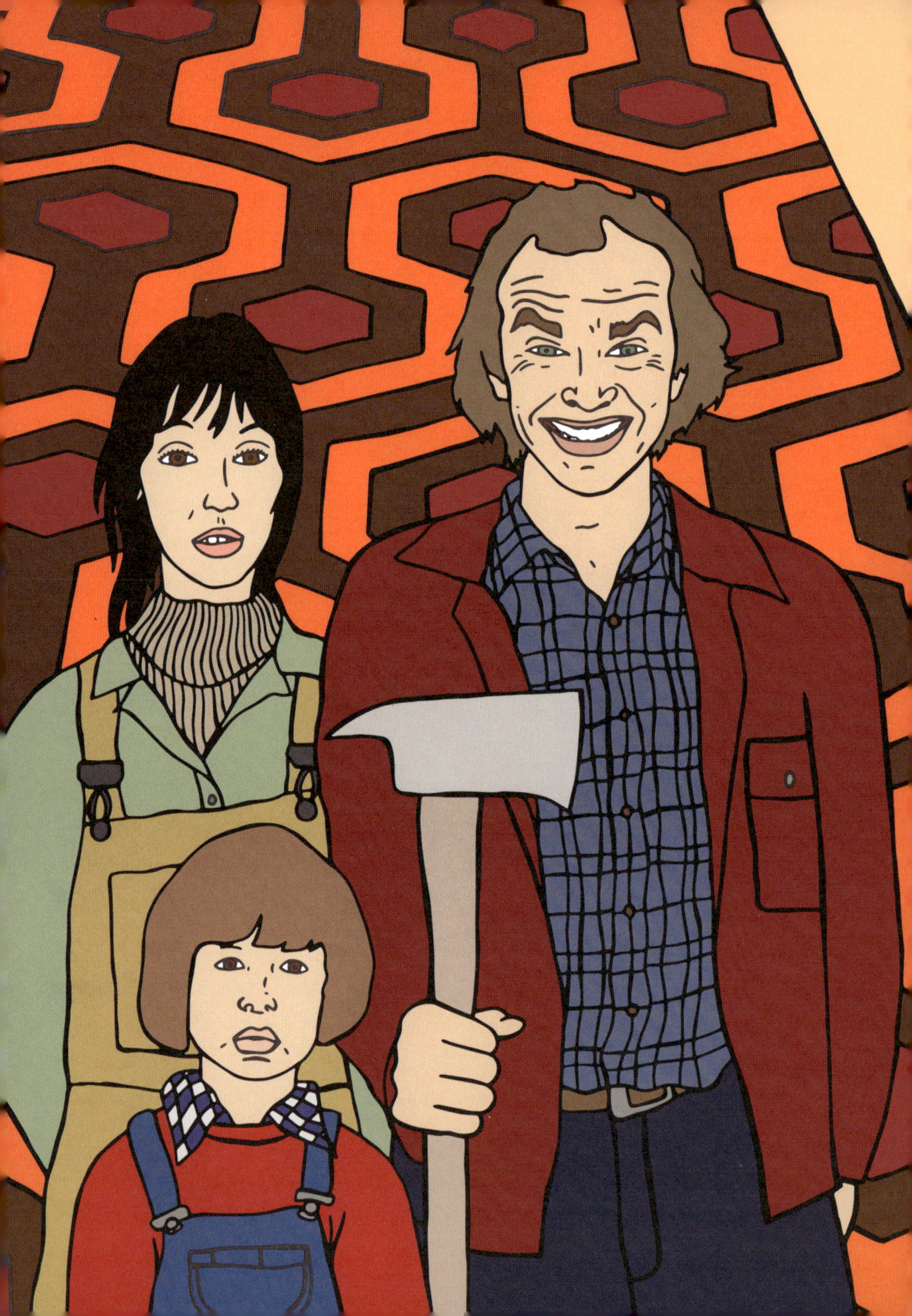

Trips with kids are **stressful**,
they'll make you
lose your mind.

Just leave the hatchet
back at home,
and it'll be **alright**.

Then there's **Bowser Jr.**—
now **his** old man's an asshole.

A **deadbeat dad,**
off hiding Peach
inside another castle.

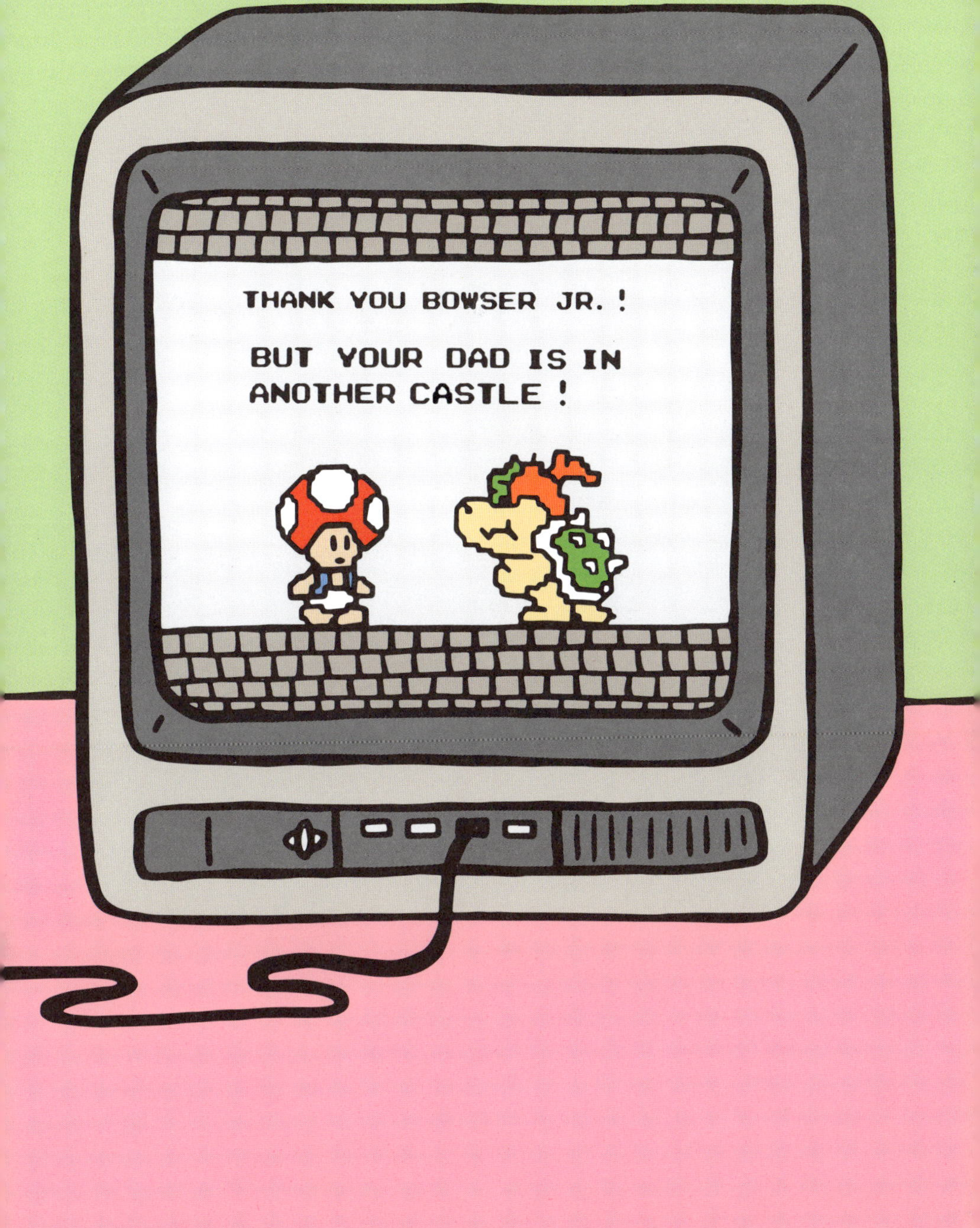
THANK YOU BOWSER JR. !
BUT YOUR DAD IS IN
ANOTHER CASTLE !

—24—

Pharaoh Akhenaten,

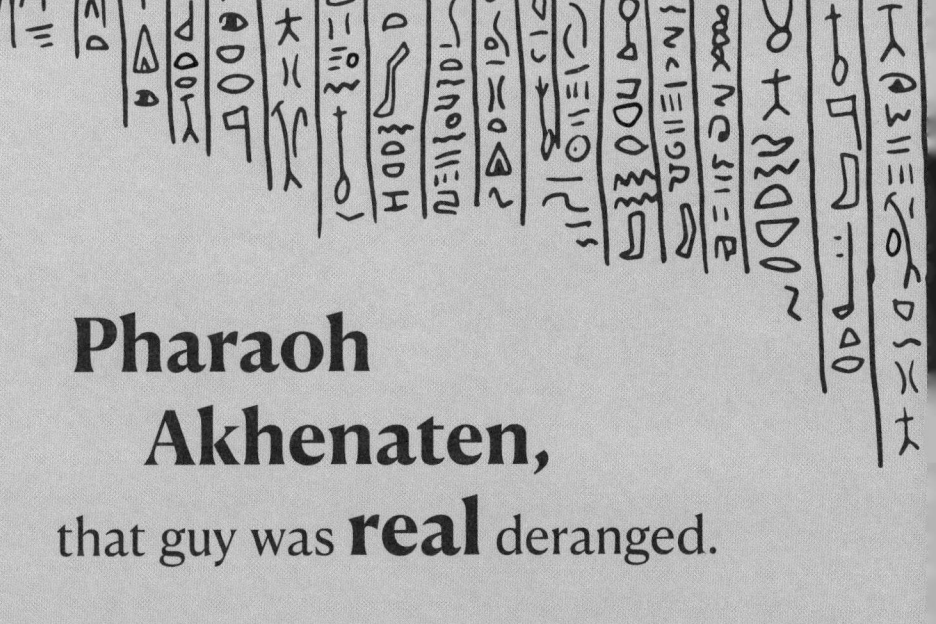

that guy was **real** deranged.

His son—**King Tut!**—was so ashamed, he had his own name changed.

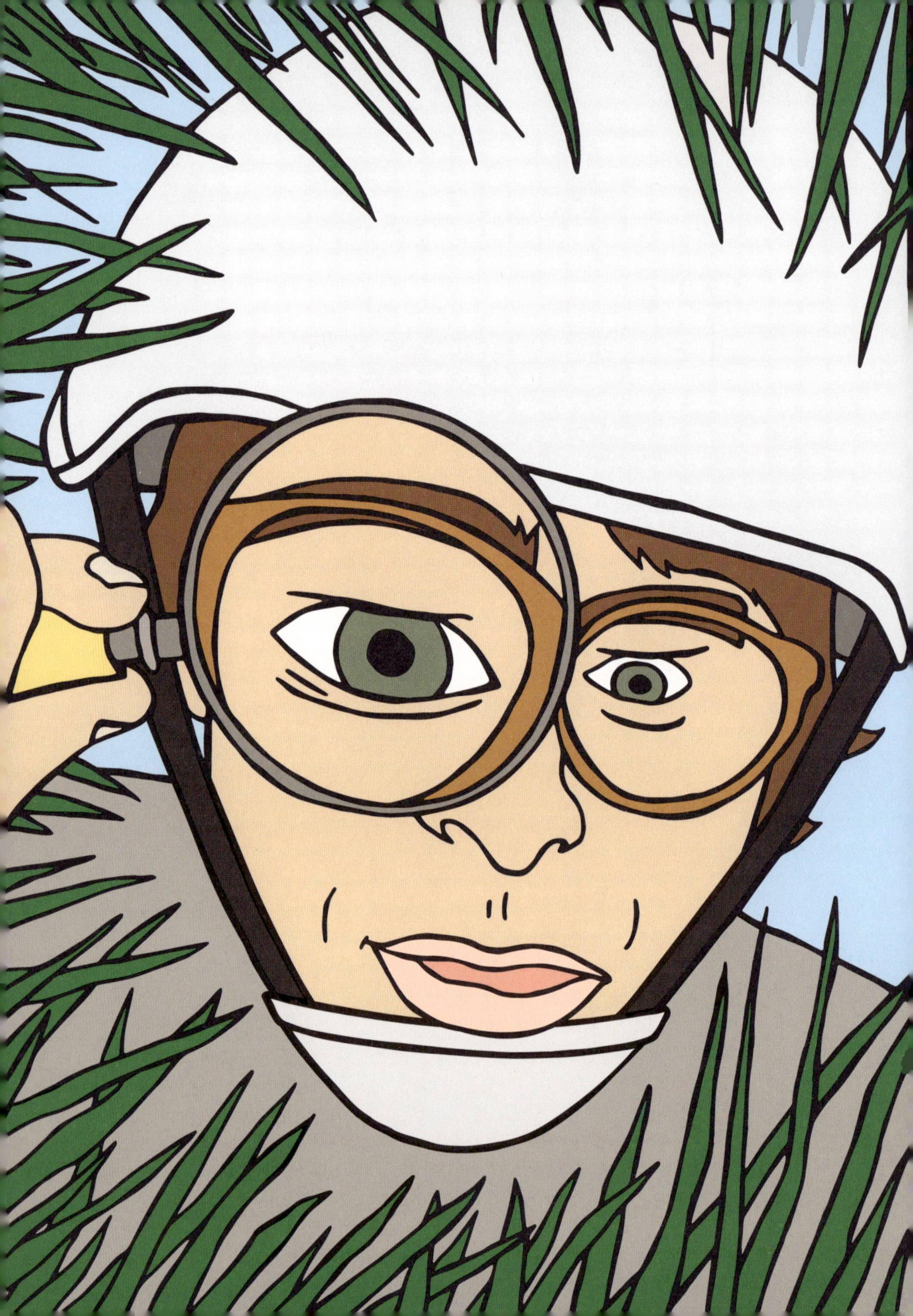

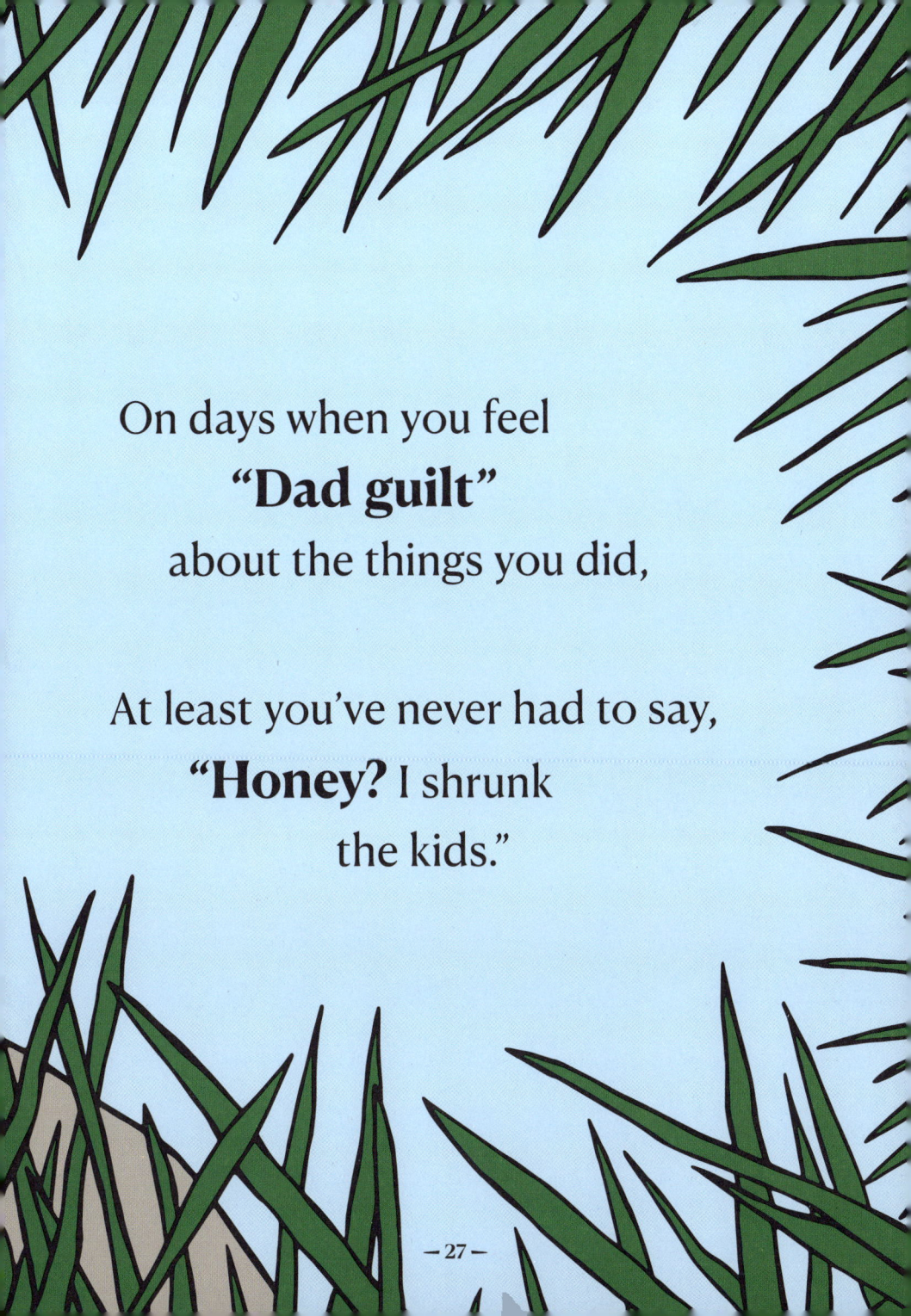

On days when you feel
"Dad guilt"
about the things you did,

At least you've never had to say,
"Honey? I shrunk
the kids."

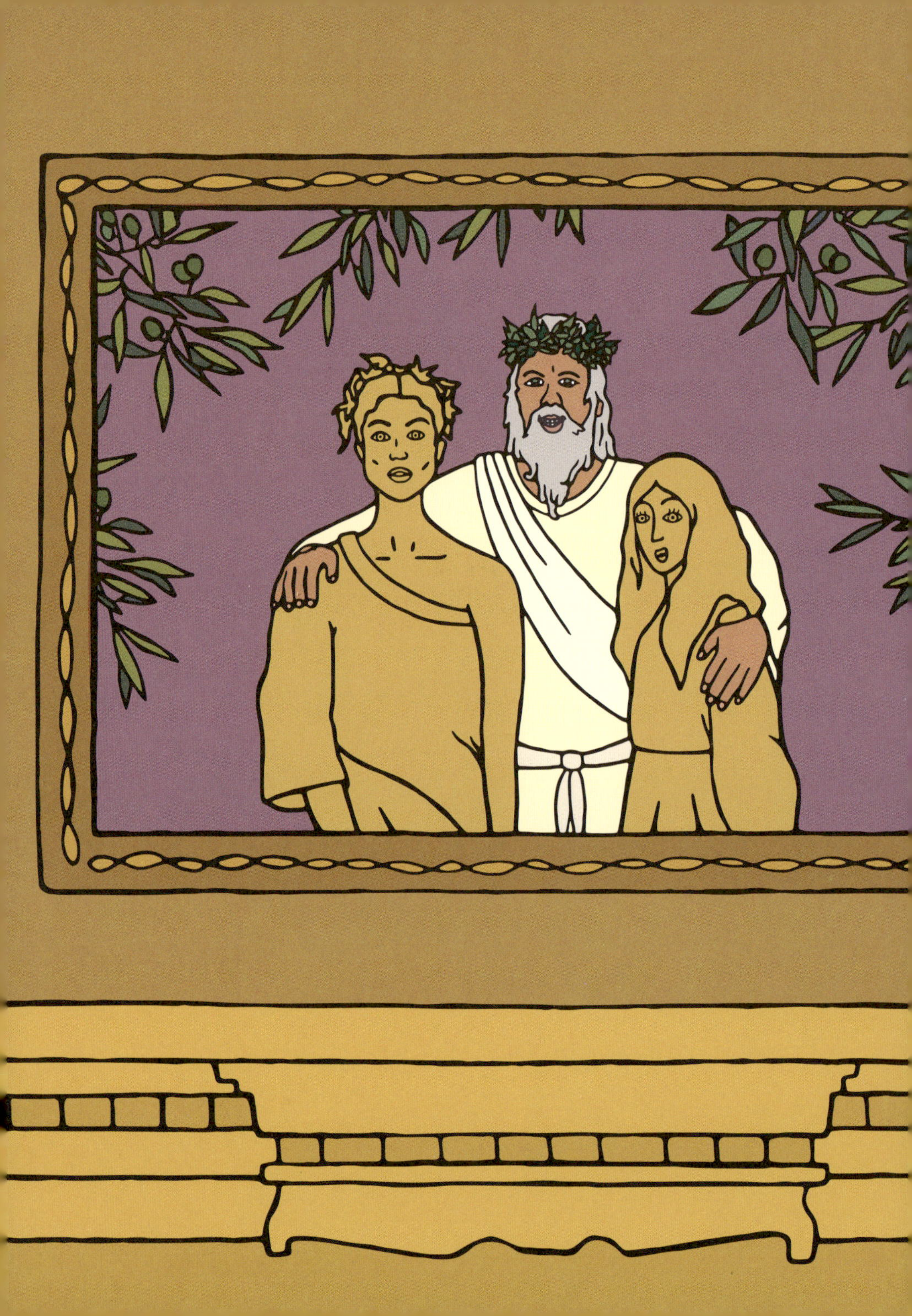

Poor dad? Rich dad?
In between?
Nobody's gonna care.

Midas had the golden touch
and look what
happened there.

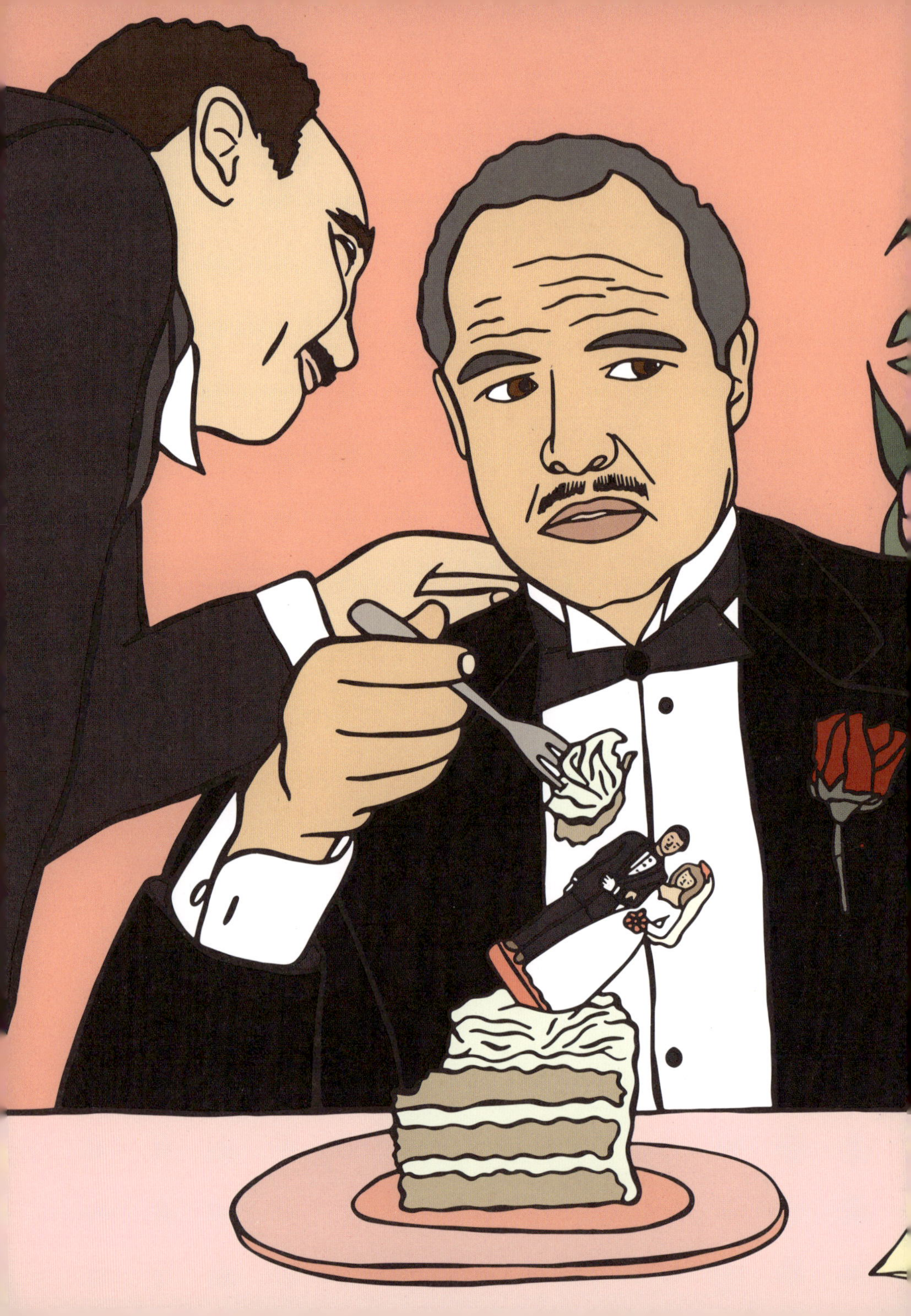

For dads who feel they **"work too much,"** before you start a-fretting,

The **Godfather** took business meetings at his daughter's wedding.

Poor kid **Harry Osborn,**
his pop's an awful one—

Too busy hunting Spider-Man to spend time with his **son.**

Lord Tywin

from *Game of Thrones?*
Oh man, his kids were **bitter.**

Take comfort in
 the fact yours haven't
killed you on
 the shitter.

The Raven
POLITICS: NOT GOOD
HODOR SPEAKS "HODOR."
Style Section
Our Favorite Chainmail
SUDOKU
WEATHER REPORT:
M T W T F

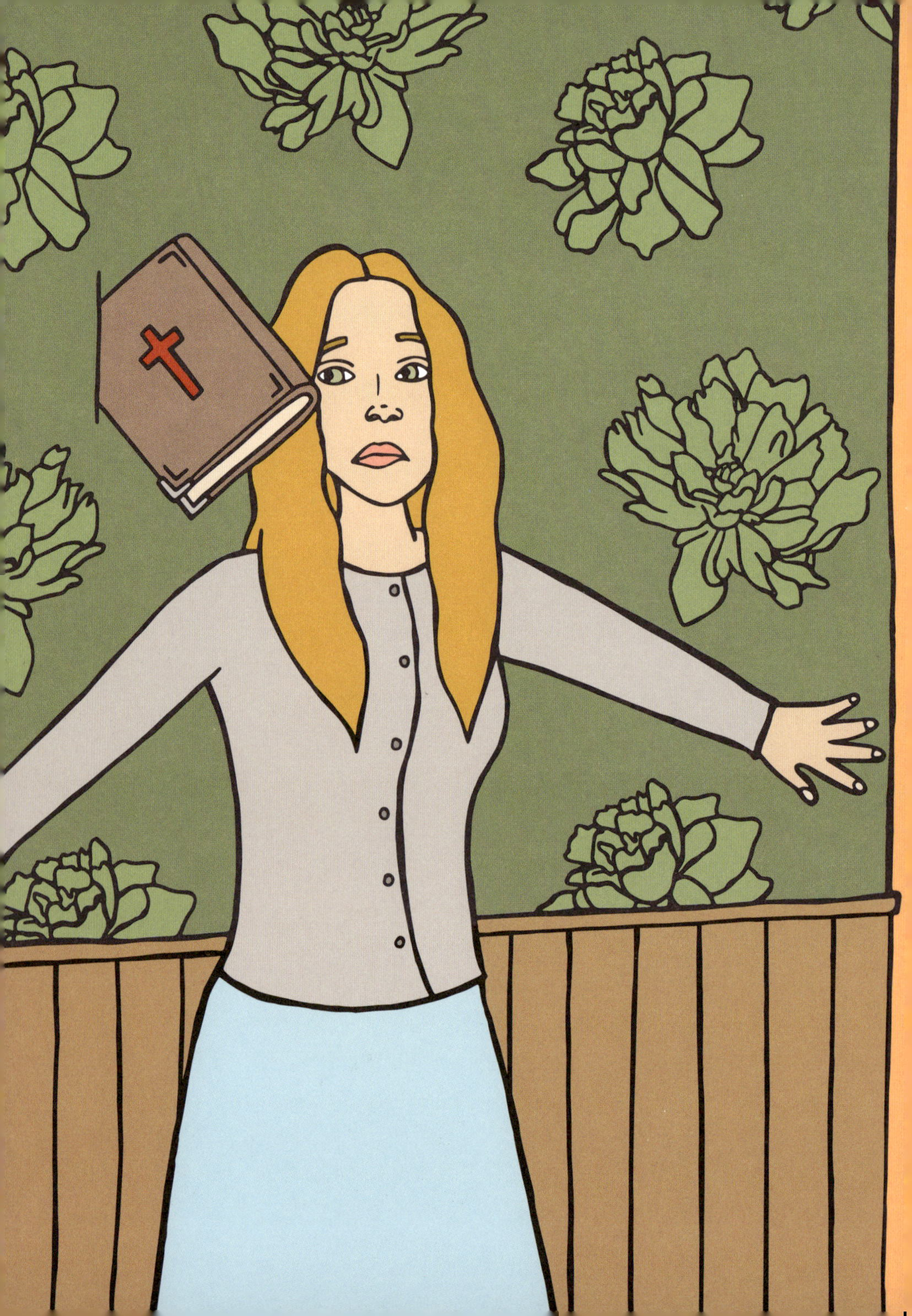

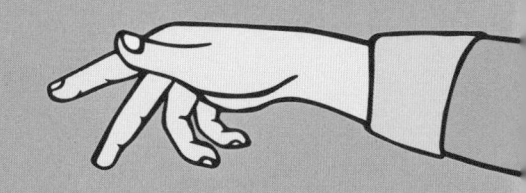

Dads can suck,
   as we've all seen . . .
   but moms are also liable.

Carrie's mom
   thought she was cursed
   and smacked her
      with **a Bible.**

Norma Bates from *Psycho* gave her son **too** much love.

So he took to **stabbing** pretty ladies in the tub.

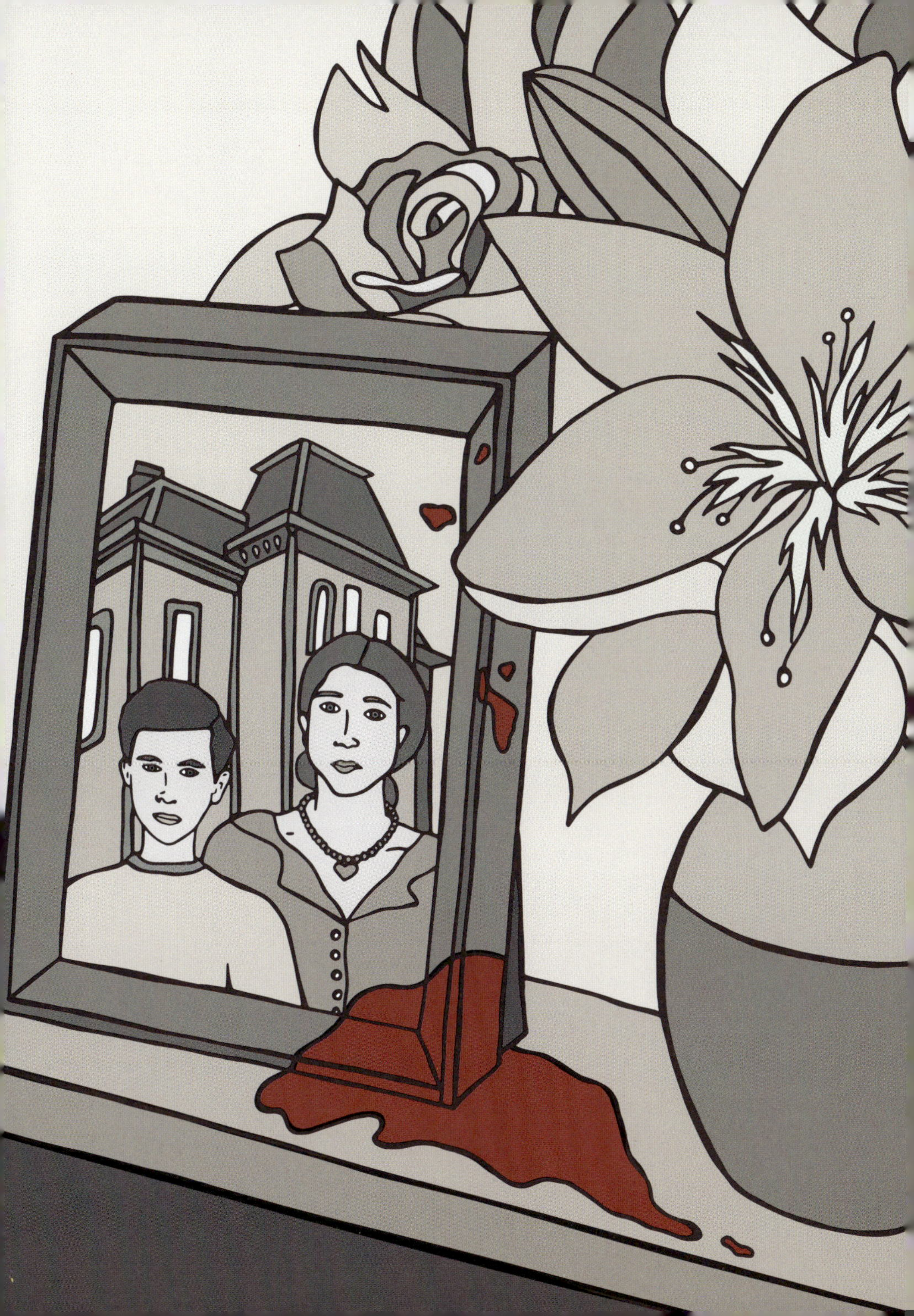

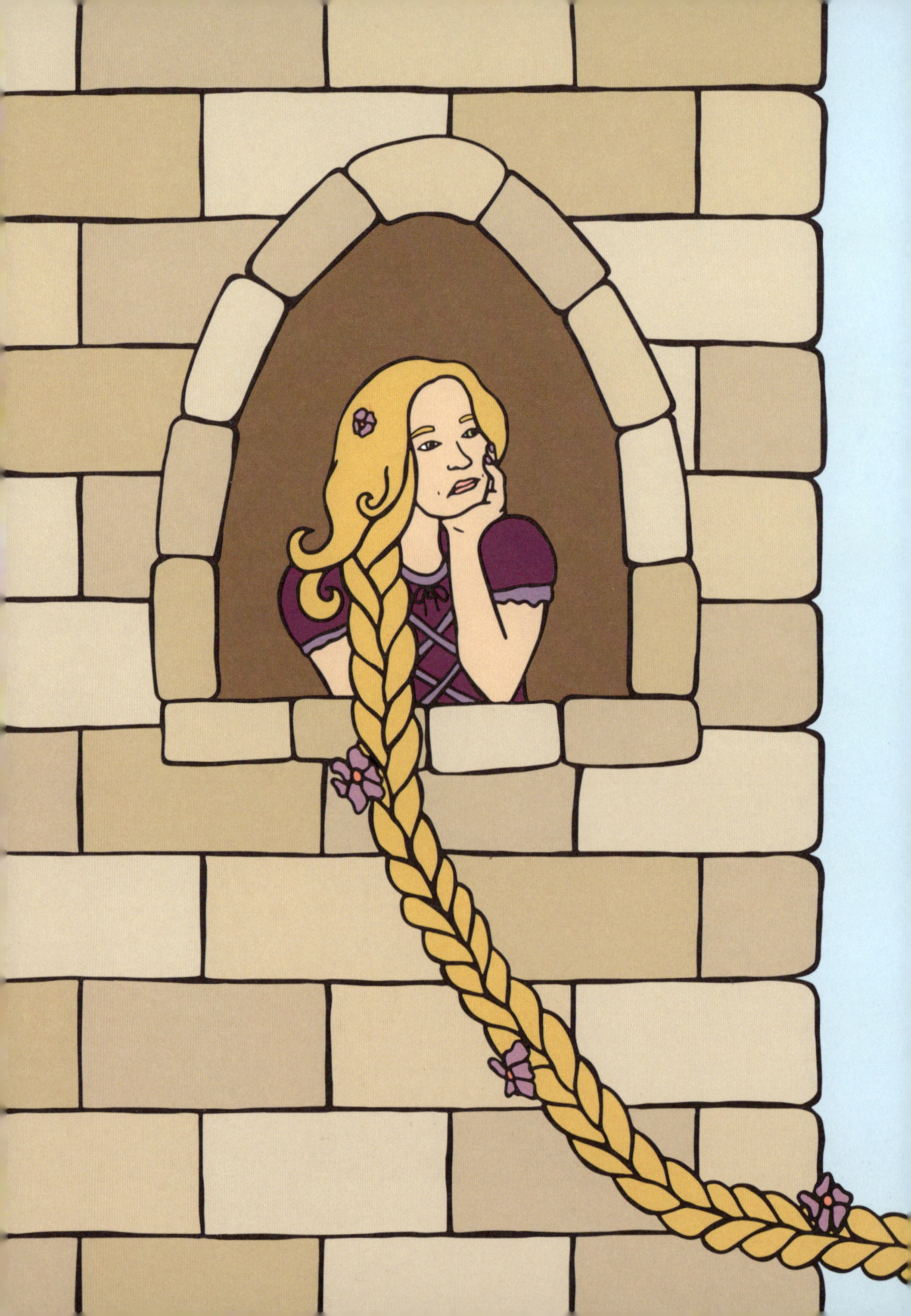

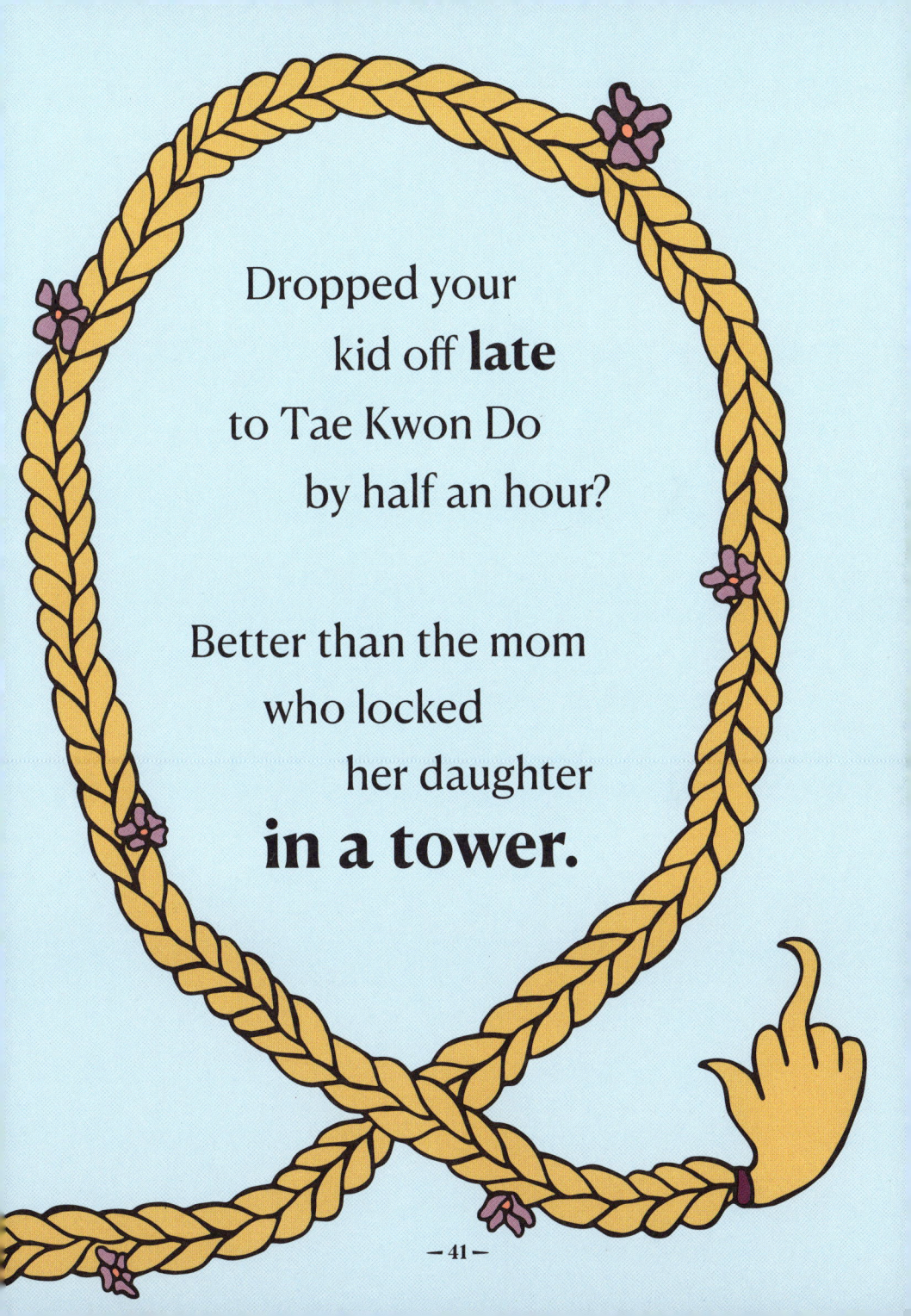

Dropped your kid off **late** to Tae Kwon Do by half an hour?

Better than the mom who locked her daughter **in a tower.**

Both adults
from *Home Alone?*
By all accounts, **quite nice.**

But they forgot
their son at home.
In fact, they
did it **twice.**

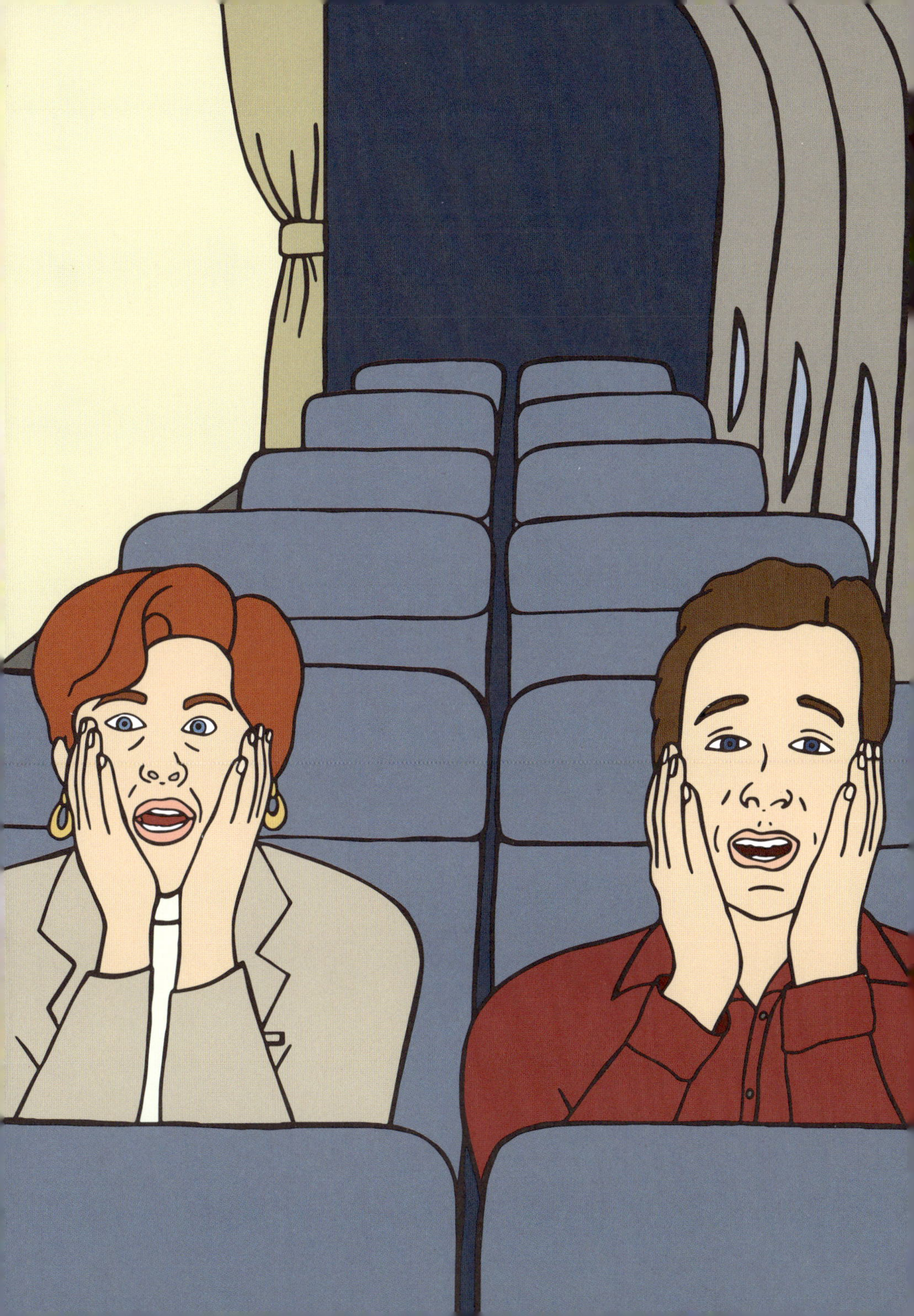

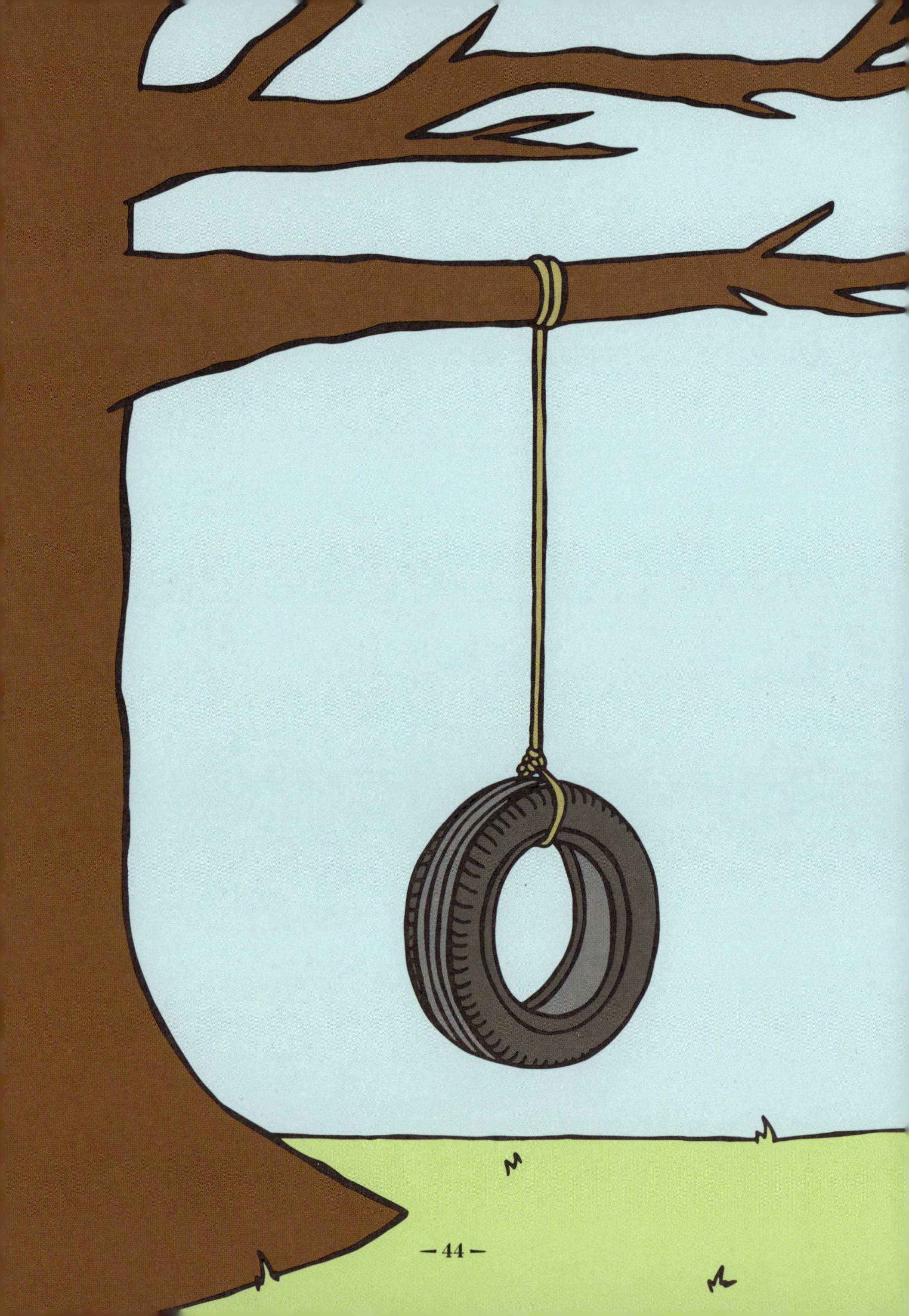

Honestly, there will be times
you feel like World's Worst Dad.
But when it comes to having kids,
mistakes are often had.

They'll **fall from trees**
and skin their knees
and fail their science test.

They'll climb on shelves
and **burn themselves**
and steal from CVS.

They'll play their music **way too loud** and dye their hair too bright.

They'll **talk back** when you ground them and you'll end up in a fight.

They'll **sneak out**
after midnight,
go streaking in the dark.

They'll kiss on dates
and **fall in love**
and nurse a broken heart.

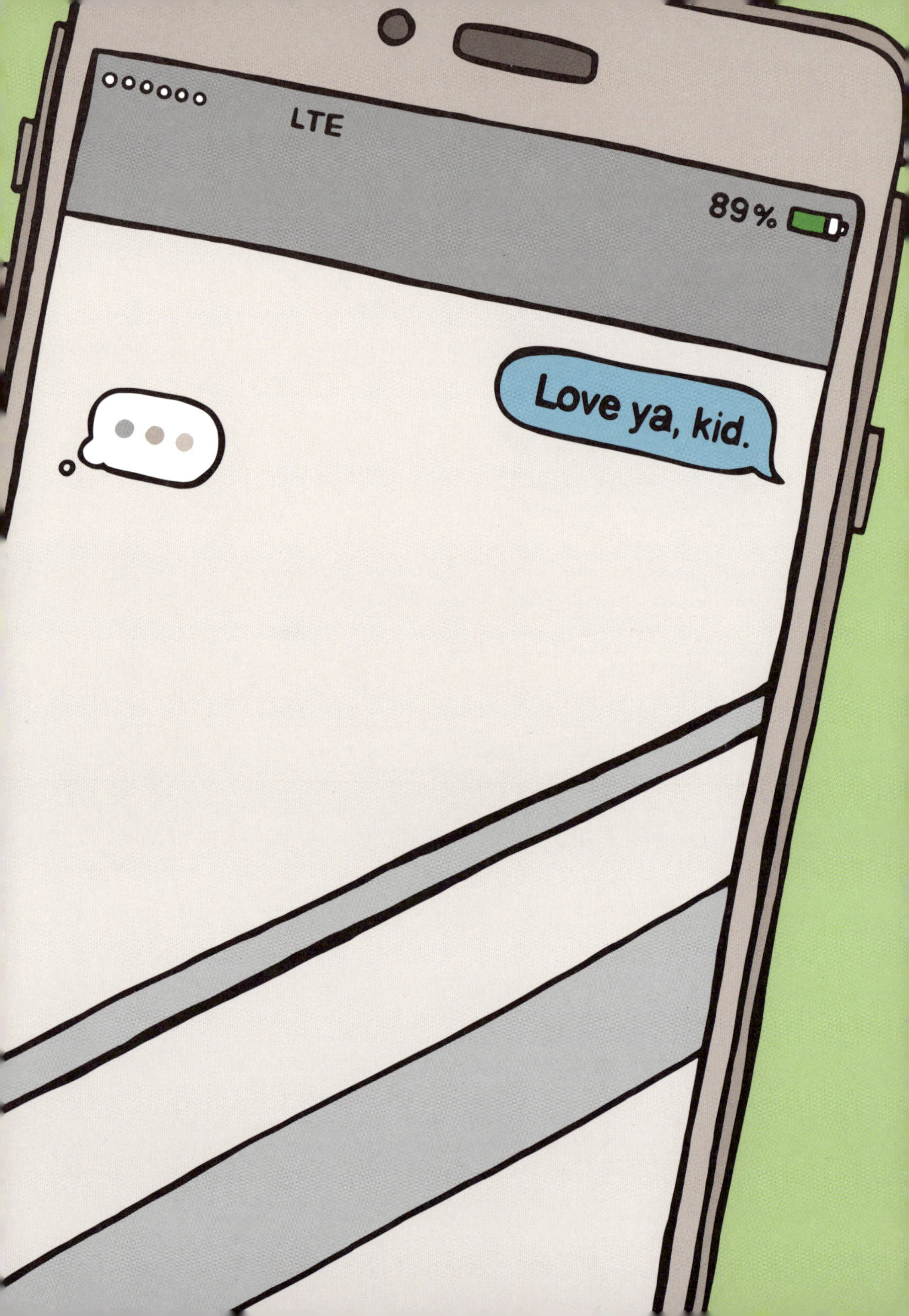
LTE
89%
Love ya, kid.

And though you
 can't protect them
as they spread their wings to fly,

You'll be right there
to **catch them**
and hold them when they cry.

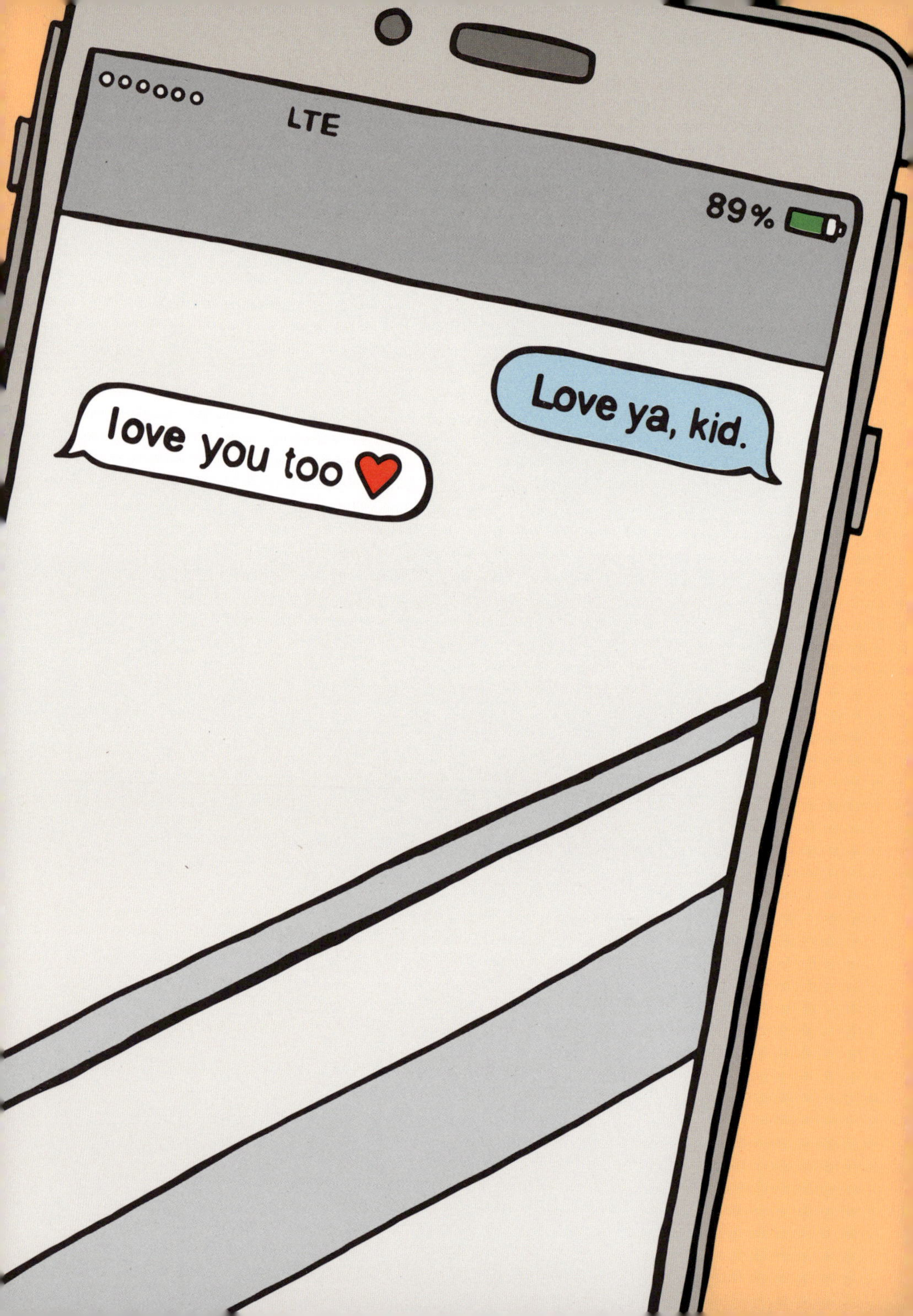
LTE
89%
Love ya, kid.
love you too

You might not make
 the Guinness Book
for parenting **the best,**

But even so,
 your kid believes
you're **better** than the rest.

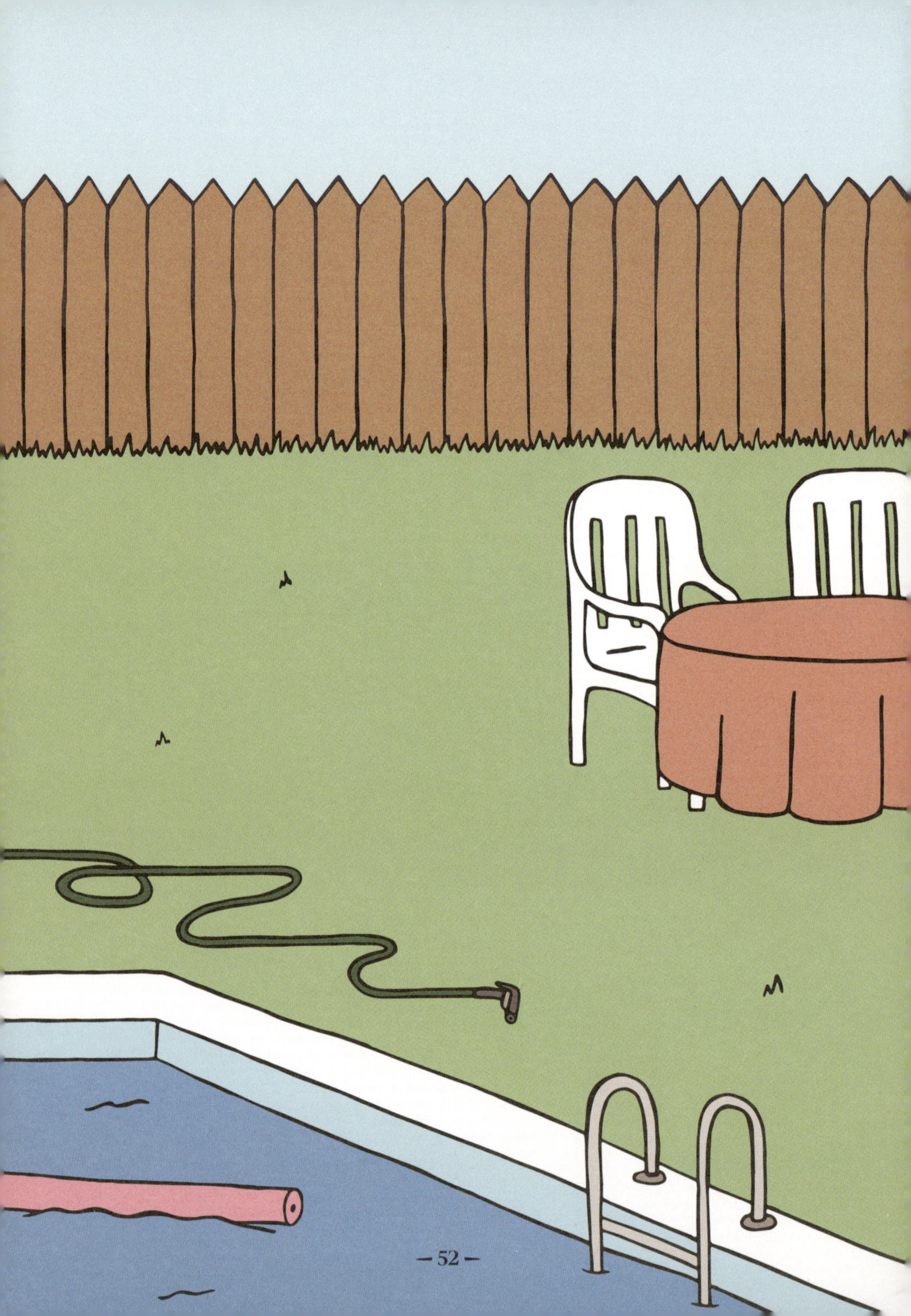

So on those days
when nothing's right and
everything feels **cursed,**

Just know that when
it comes to dads…

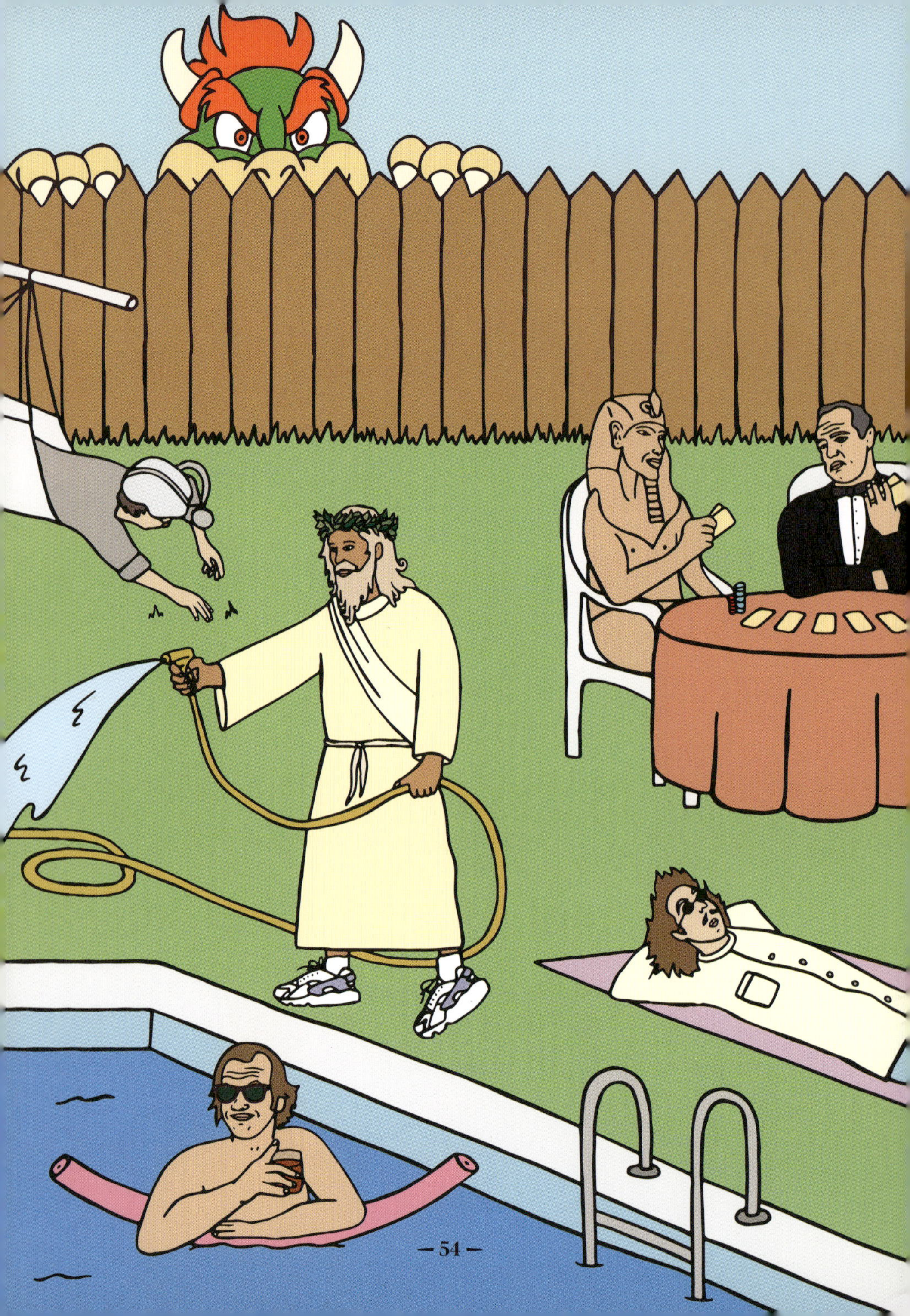

...you'll never be the worst!

APPENDIX

Whether these terrible dads and moms are misguided, misunderstood, or just plain evil, a more nuanced (and, perhaps, kinder) analysis proves they're just parenting the only way they know how.

Thanos

Thanos, an original character in the Marvel Universe, is best known as the purple guy who's obsessed with collecting jewelry. To debate which version of him counts as canon would take longer than an Avengers movie, but one thing is certain across every film, comic, and time line: He's a shitty dad.

In the cinematic universe, Thanos would say his daughters Nebula and Gamora are "adopted," while others might say he "kept them as souvenirs after genocide-ing their respective planets." Thanos views his children as tools to achieve his goals and is obsessed with molding them into powerful assassins. When they were young, Thanos regularly forced his daughters to fight each other. But Nebula often lost, so to "improve" her, he tortured her and turned her into a cyborg. Tough love, perhaps? He wasn't much nicer to Gamora, though: in *Avengers: Infinity War*, Thanos pushed her off a cliff in exchange for the Soul Stone, which helps him gain the ability to destroy half of the universe in a single snap.

Walter White

Walter White (aka "Heisenberg") is the lead character in the television series *Breaking Bad*, and one of TV's best antiheroes. The chemistry-teacher-turned-meth-chef certainly had his bad dad moments. Like, ya know, becoming a drug lord and embroiling his family in a web of criminal activity, culminating in the death of his son's uncle and eventually himself. But, through a more sympathetic lens, Mr. White's original intention was to *improve* his children's lives. After all, as Walter tearily says to Walter Jr. in the series' penultimate episode: "I wanted to give you so much more."

Darth Vader

Decades before Maury Povich, George Lucas was surprising audiences with paternity results. Notable among his many dad crimes, Sith Lord Darth Vader explodes his daughter Leia's adopted home planet of Alderaan while forcing her to watch. He also famously cuts off his son Luke's hand with a lightsaber.

Even so, some Star Wars fans would argue Vader isn't a "bad" dad. He's just . . . passionate. Like Walter White (see previous), the whole reason Darth Vader turns to villainy in the first place is to help save his family. Eventually, Vader even gets a final moment of paternal redemption: His love for Luke turns Vader back to the Light Side, right before he sacrifices himself to save his son.

Doctor Frankenstein

In January 1818, a publishing house in London printed 500 copies of a little book called *Frankenstein; or, The Modern Prometheus*. Since then, there have been over 300 published editions. Though there have been varying depictions of Frankenstein's Monster (bolts in neck, bolts in forehead, bolt-free), the original story is essentially that of a deadbeat dad: Doctor Victor Frankenstein creates life, realizes he's in over his head, and spends a big part of the story avoiding any parental responsibility. This, in turn, causes his technically newborn son to lash out in the form of murdering people, simply to get his dad's attention.

Some men just aren't ready to be fathers—so in many ways, *Frankenstein* can be interpreted as an endorsement for birth control.

Jack Torrance

Work/life balance is difficult for any parent, especially if you have a child with creepy supernatural powers. But for Jack Torrance in *The Shining*, that's still no excuse to try and chop up your son in a hedge maze. There's no telling what kind of real-life trauma an experience like that would inflict, but child actor Danny Lloyd wasn't fazed while filming it. According to Lloyd (who was five years old at the time), he didn't even know *The Shining* was a horror movie. To keep him from getting too scared, he was told they were making a drama. In fact, he didn't see the film until he was sixteen.

Bowser

There are two ways to interpret Bowser's approach to parenting: One, he's a taskmaster who forces his son, Bowser Jr., to carry out his villainous errands without proper compensation. Two, Bowser is just a struggling single dad, taking any opportunity he can to bond with his son. Either way you slice it, he's putting his kid to work.

Nintendo introduced Bowser Jr. in 2002's *Super Mario Sunshine*. In the game, Bowser lies to his son and claims Peach is his biological mother. (According to official lore, Mario

— 57 —

creator Shigeru Miyamoto says nobody knows who Bowser Jr.'s mother is). Since then, Bowser Jr. has walked through lava, smashed, and bombed in order to win his father's approval. Their relationship is less "Father/Son" and more "Supervillain/Minion."

Pharaoh Akhenaten

Akhenaten—or more famously, King Tut's dad—is one of ancient history's most unpopular pharaohs. His reign lasted for about seventeen years during the eighteenth dynasty of the New Kingdom. During his rule, Akhenaten pissed off everyone in Egypt because he tried to shift society from a polytheistic to a more monotheistic religion (but, like, whose dad hasn't?). So, when his heir, King Tut, finally took the throne, Tut thought it would be best to distance himself from his father's trainwreck of a reign. He dropped the "Aten" from his birth name (Tutankh*aten*) and became the Tutankh*amun*, "Amun," referring to one of the traditional gods his father tried to eradicate.

Wayne Szalinski

Honey, I Shrunk the Kids is a tale as old as time: Scatterbrained inventor creates a molecule-altering laser that accidentally shrinks his children and their friends, who then enlist the help of an ant to escape their backyard until they eventually fall into a bowl of cereal and are nearly consumed. If this plot sounds dramatic, it's because it was: The movie was originally conceived as a drama. Less than three weeks before filming, writer Tom Schulman was hired to retool the entire script as a comedy. Redeeming dad quality of Mr. Szalinski: As clumsy and careless as he is, once he realizes what he's done, he will stop at nothing to resize his kids.

King Midas

The ancient myth recounts the cautionary tale of greedy King Midas, who wishes for the Golden Touch, then can't eat food because he turns it all to gold. His daughter didn't become part of the story until Nathaniel Hawthorne wrote her into his version in 1852: Midas hugs his daughter and accidentally turns her into solid metal, as well. So, while Midas' golden touch dates back to ancient times, his bad paternal instincts were acquired more recently. But some scholars believe the story *is* based on a real guy from the eighth century BCE: a wealthy royal, "Mita of Mushki," who ruled over the Phrygian region in what is now present-day Turkey. It's theorized his clothing might have been the inspiration for the myth. Through chemical analysis, archaeologists discovered that many upper-class garments in Mita's time were coated in iron oxide, which would have made them appear gold in color.

Don Vito Corleone

For someone with "God" and "Father" in their name, you'd think this guy would be a decent dad. Arms dealing, extortion, theft, and murder aside, Don Vito Corleone couldn't even bother to take *one* day off from work to celebrate his only daughter's nuptials. However, *The Godfather* director, Francis Ford Coppola, had a much better relationship with his own dad. Coppola cast his father, Carmine, in the movie. He can be spotted as the mafia bar piano player during the "Gang Wars" montage sequence.

Norman Osborn

Next time you feel like a bad father, remember you haven't tried blowing up your son's best friend with Pumpkin Bombs.

Like Thanos, Norman Osborn is a workaholic father from the Marvel Universe who regularly puts his own ambitions above the well-being of his children. It's slightly more understandable when Osborn neglects his parenting while embodying his supervillain alter ego, the Green Goblin (when he transforms, his mental chemistry is altered). But he's not even that great a dad when he's regular Norman Osborn; in most iterations of the Spider-Man story, Norman—something of a scientist himself—often expresses his disappointment in his not-scientist son Harry and prefers the company of fellow nerd (and Spider-Man), Peter Parker.

Tywin Lannister

For those who have only seen *Game of Thrones* on TV, you'll be delighted to know Lord Tywin Lannister is just as bad a father in the books. From calling his daughter stupid, to bullying his son Jamie about his dyslexia, to ordering his guards to assault his daughter-in-law, Tywin is a real piece of shit. One of the real-life inspirations for Lord Lannister is thought to be King Edward I, a figure so intimidating, it's rumored he once scared a servant to death.

Margaret White

In the 1976 movie *Carrie*, Carrie's mom might have been a nutty religious fundamentalist who thought her daughter was possessed . . . but she also wasn't totally wrong. Her daughter *did* have supernatural powers. Call it maternal instinct. Could Margaret have handled the news differently and not stabbed her daughter in the back with a kitchen knife on prom night? Sure. But it also made for a great film; *Carrie* went on to be one of the most popular horror movies of all time, inspiring a sequel, multiple reboots, and even a 1988 musical (that closed after five days).

Norma Bates

Norma Bates' obsession with her only son was, to put it nicely, perverse. In the words of Norman himself: "A son is a poor substitute for a lover." Norma fostered such a codependent relationship, in fact, that when she started dating a new man, Norman murdered him—and then her—in a fit of jealousy, then taxidermized her body so they could still "hang out." Is that love or insanity? Who's to say?

Psycho author Robert Bloch said, when writing Norman, he took inspiration from serial killer Ed Gein. Gein also had a strict mom whose draconian attitude toward sex inspired him to murder young women. After all . . . "A boy's best friend is his mother."

Rapunzel's Godmother

Rapunzel is the story of a long-haired, indoor kid whose "adoptive" witch mom (aka Dame Gothel) keeps her locked in a tower. But actually, the witch isn't the story's only villain: In the Grimm Brothers version from 1812, a pregnant woman spots a type of vegetable (called rapunzel!) in her witchy neighbor's garden, and exclaims she needs it to satisfy her pregnancy cravings. Instead of just, oh, I dunno, *asking* the witch, the husband steals some. He gets caught, and in exchange for leniency agrees to let the witch have his firstborn daughter . . . without clearing it with his wife first. It's comforting to know that behind every bad mom is an equally bad dad.

Kate and Peter McCallister

Home Alone is the David and Goliath tale of how one brave young man protects his home from burglars. It's also about two overwhelmed parents who accidentally forget their son at home on a family trip to Paris. But traveling with children (eleven, in the case of the McCallisters) is stressful.

In a 2021 study from NYU, "Eighty-eight percent of parents are likely or very likely to travel with their children in the next twelve months." In another study, the data shows that the average American must return home *four times a month* because they forgot something. There's no data on whether those things are human children, but the point is: If you forget your kids at home, don't be so hard on yourself.

ACKNOWLEDGMENTS

Thank you to the fellow co-parents of this book: Brandi Bowles, Reg Tigerman, Megan Nicolay, Jessica Weil, Galen Smith, Beth Levy, Annie O'Donnell, Barbara Peragine, Doug Wolff, and the rest of the brilliant Workman team.

Thank you to Jared Logan and the kind, patient souls who explained Star Wars lore to me: Matthew Chiaramonte, Shaun Diston, Julieanne Smolinski, and John Timothy.

Thank you to the Good Dads in my life: Dad, Gagey, Joe, and Reeshard.

Last but not least, John Danek. I love you!

ABOUT THE AUTHOR

GLENN BOOZAN is an Emmy-nominated and WGA Award-winning comedy writer whose credits include—among others—*CONAN*, *Home Economics*, and Sarah Silverman's *I Love You, America*. In a shocking twist, she's also the author of *There Are Moms Way Worse Than You*, a *New York Times* besteller.

ABOUT THE ILLUSTRATOR

PRISCILLA WITTE is a Los Angeles–based illustrator and muralist whose work has taken her across the globe. Her partnerships include Warner Music Group, Twitch, Masterclass, Mattel (Barbie), and Google—and she recently painted seven murals in the arts district of Los Angeles. In an extraordinary coincidence, she's also the illustrator of the *New York Times* bestselling book *There Are Moms Way Worse Than You*.